D1202590

Blight, Blight, Blight, Ray of Hope

Blight, Blight, Blight, Ray of Hope

Frank Montesonti

I wish they would put a shot of whiskey next to the Bible.

Frank

Barrow Street Press
New York City

Designed by Robert Drummond

Cover photography by Geoff Wilson

Published by Barrow Street Press
Distributed by:
      Barrow Street Books
      P.O. Box 1558
      Kingston, RI 02881

First Edition

Library of Congress Control Number: 2012942001

ISBN 978-0-9819876-7-5

CONTENTS

The Incalculably Long Geometry of Sobriety

November always starts out this way:

You feel like a box; then you feel trapped in a box.

A week since my last drink. The falling from the high blue
       I was, was
more crystalline in the memory than climbing spiral
apartment staircases in Chicago.
                It's called *a flight of stairs*
because you're rising. You feel like a movie,
rapping on someone's door;

then you're in a movie;
you could swing the camera around and watch the
       brickwork of snow.

I'm going to miss the winter,
how it throws a white sheet over the lawns and caps
the trash cans. How it expects

us to wait like starved doves under a magician's cape
for the disappearing. It will hurt the first time you look

at the winter and *the winter in us.*

Out there in the snow is a kid in a blue sweater with a head
       full of bronze gears
who is trying to grasp the incalculably long geometry
of loss and life. I'll miss him too.

But not having the shakes so bad,
stumbling by bungalow-style houses spiked with ice,
it seemed the world would shatter.

Today, under the cold

and overcast sky I go to the laundry room to buy
        another soda.
O Loneliness.
I love the staged heartbeat of a Coke shouldered
        from the machine.

Redundancy of Light

Outside this hotel room
rain falls as pure as its definition.
Call the French; tell them

there should be a word
for shadows of raindrops
on a hotel window.

Scientists say that if you could hear your own
heartbeat you'd slowly go insane.
I lie on the floor and the shadow rain

moves over my skin as I listen
to something bigger than my one heart:

billions of people
and their loneliness
rising like humidity.

I wish they would put a shot of whiskey
next to the Bible
in every hotel drawer
so I could warm to the idea
of living forever.

More shadows, more rain,
a pump, bigger and as constant,
that I can't turn off.

Trees step out of their shadows.
A few cars make incisions in the skin of water
on the road, but they heal.

They always heal. If, I mean when,
you also realize yours
is the only heartbeat you cannot hear,

I need to tell you something before it's too late:
It's too late.

A Flock of Iagos Waiting in the Wings

On a bridge in Indianapolis
I'm getting covered with coils of snow
like George Bailey—Jimmy Stewart—in *It's
a Wonderful Life*, before he wishes he

was never born and then is swallowed
whole by an alternate universe
like a snake unhinging its jaw to admit
even the bones. So, sans George, the ursine

winter took his brother's life; the druggist
went to prison for dispensing rat poison
instead of aspirin; and no kindly bank
offered affordable mortgages, so the town

was constricted financially, then choked
out by cheep neon from the luminous
vices. Every time I watch the film my heart
feels like Lucifer in a tree when I realize

that, just because George reneges on his wish,
this whole other earth will be erased;
the decent-man-turned-snake-oil–salesman,
high on gin, will lose the brief venom

of a *Live Girls* sign, when George
is born again. I read this article
about some scientists who theorized
twenty ways the world might end,

and the last way was: Someone wakes up
and finds it has all been a dream. Yes, this trick
is cheap soap opera tripe, but who says
we live in an expensive universe? On *NOVA*

I saw the story of a man with a condition
called the Capgras Delusion who believed
all his loved ones were carbon-copy imposters.
He wasn't frightened; he didn't think his parents

were reptiles in rubber suits or Iagos waiting
in the wings, rubbing their elderly hands;
they just weren't *them*. He even referred
to himself as the *other* David. I'm standing

on a bridge in Indianapolis watching the legless
moonlight, the legless snow, snake
through the wind, worried the marriage might
carry off the ether that holds us down.

In the winter this is a humorless city,
and behind me cars strike through the slush.
I'm not thinking of doing anything drastic;
I'm just watching the light from the nearby power

plant occasionally coil in a divot of water,
shine like a scale, and then disappear.

Heaven's Undershirt

Imagine a beach where the waves fold into curls of damaged
brightness and white houses stretch down the hill to a kind
of eternity. I'm there, a shape abstract enough to be all I
remember in this life. Hail thwacks on umbrellas. Hail
rebounding off the street making long skewed check marks.

Impressionistic swirls of daybreak through window screens.
Noise pooled in the divots of sand. A blackbird on the
cleaning table lifts the skin of a walleye.

My dreams begin in an overgrown field in Indiana. Fireflies
spark in staccato flashes. Then the dark churns out FACES.
In my dreams:

a diamond as big as a car.

Noise shot from a finite point. The sky steers the earth.
A hand emerges from the noise, then a silhouette, then my
jacket of cold. The waves broke into white static at the bar.
Walking down the beach we looked like quarter notes from
a distance.

Raindrops hit our skin, undid the old photographs in their
bellies on the cool sand. A gull cried; *space smells like a fired gun*.

Something justifying about this beach, this lie, this hunger of
gulls making strong brushstrokes above the sailboats' right
triangles. The wind twined your hair into a lucent shape.

Our footsteps trailed behind us, then pushed their
signatures out.

My mother washing lake water off her hands with tap water,
cold and distant as herself. Each of the thousand lakes divines
the vague blue of all things transitory, and she thinks she can
work herself clean.

It's almost as if I'm in a place not quite a place, heaven almost. When you turn on a lamp, stars are silent. Resting your head on the cold car window. Christmas trees in living rooms. Smell of gasoline in the marina.

Imagine Chicago. The same ejaculating fountain in the same arc and the birds all hung with feathers and the sky all hung with birds. Lives are silence. Only one light is on in death.

The crayon picture you drew of the two men carrying so many rifles up the hill they could have been dying metaphorically.

The El rattles pans from cheap studios. Go back to the beach. No, don't. Rivers keep flowing, and some lesser-known fraction comes to dominate the future.

*
*
*

Dear Reader. One night when I was still becoming a man, the moon threw down its white, wet underclothes on the tree branches in my front yard

And since then I've been shocked.

So I tried to forget. To float away. A hiss of dark
         liquid and I'd join the sky.
I don't love myself.

Two lawn chairs so close they're kissing. Traveling cross-country I imagined the old Volvo that passed had a bumper sticker that read, "Death Tastes Like Vanilla Wafers."

In the heart of man is how he disappears, holds

himself to fault and faults and loves the world too much.
Locking up the store, smoking, the dumpster
smoking in the winter air, the factories' big cigarettes.

A Cheetos bag flung against my leg outside the Arby's,
and I sat down right there and thought about all the
parking lots in the world.

The lake has layers of cold. Hook a leach through its head.
My Bears jacket is flimsy. Half of the pockets of water are
filled with silver; others move in a darkness I must still
be coming to terms with.

The way an indoor pool opens like an orchid does with
          wavy blue light on the ceiling.
If it's not too much to ask, I'd like to know something
about you, something dark. What motorcycle stunt would
your heart be?

Easy. The woman in the sphere with the six cycles. Easy.
As you filed past me for the basketball game I could smell
vanilla following you.

In the library is a book called The *Third Treasury of the
Familiar*, and nowhere in the book will you find a charcoal
sketch of your heart, of the little black drunken skeleton
flung again and again against the wall of your ventricle.
Listen closer.

In the courtyard of my friend's apartment in Hollywood
while reading a book light fell on the page of verse and I
read what was underneath. Someone in their apartment
was singing.

In an abandoned Sears parking lot I found a note; it read,
I wish you were here but I'm glad you're not. And I continued
watching the snow almost melt under the lot lights. I wrote
one back; it read, *Somewhere far away from you is another you*.

So I mistook the child by weight for the phone book.
So I left the cat on "Nap" all day.

The cup of coffee	(is)	a bomb
The falling snow	(in actuality)	someone drowning
Sorrow	(she forgot her)	red camel-hair coat on the chair.

If there are faces in the clouds, they're cold and far
away.

*
*
*

Tonight I stare into my blue eyes, at my ratty T-shirt,
my uncut haircut, into the moving of the water in that
blue, that only someone else will come to understand
as the moving of my life.

Minnesota. Trees sound their alarms. I have dreams
where I'm in a moving relief, the foreground scenery
pulled fast, the trees a little slower; the sky barely moves
at all, and these are the times I feel stuck in
narration. The nearness of nearness. Nightmares
about riding on a shrinking train.

A dog vomiting up red letters by a dead bush. No
one understands a single night of their life enough
to carve the firework back from the explosion.

You wash your hands, but you don't call it a kind
of glove. I mean, listen. A woman runs a squeegee
down the coffee-shop window, erasing the world
from the window, and all you can do is go to the
grocery store and cast your eyesight on an orange.

A crane lifts a blue box into the blue sky.

Rain makes holy static on a lake. I had a long conversation with the green cubed windshield glass on the street in the Bloomington winter moonlight until you came and touched my shoulder.

Head trauma and the smell of caged crickets in a bait shop.

I'm beginning to take the correct number of drags from my cigarette before I bend its body in half and snuff out its hair. My dreams begin in an overgrown field in Indiana, thousands of lightning bugs rising.

For in the abdomen of a lightning bug is an old man who occasionally drops his lantern. Accident nears prayer. This light rises

but does not leave the world, not quite. Night volleyball games in summer. You and I in the corner of the party, suddenly the distance between our lips, so many ellipsis dots to subtract. This light rises.

Wasp paranoia in campground restrooms. A wasp looks like an old woman pulling a black jar across ice. In this stretch of lies and birds overhead where dandelions spark in cold fields.

Pressing wet handfuls of sand through my fingers, storm clouds pulling apart in their tongue and groove above Santa Monica Pier. Your smudged silhouette in the wind almost erased. Inside man is how he disappears, flashes on this wide, wronged earth and lets his life go up and out.

The ocean looked like us all, heaved together in a dark beyond thought. Look at me on bicycle, hair tossed in scriptures, mad and sick in brown moonlight. How do you die?

How do you write about failure at all?

Every 1930s French Novel

Someone will be named Boris, and although
he is a friend he must come to be despised.
Mathieu will wash his feet before making love.
There will be much ado about Proust and crab lice.
André will see his woman, the long malaise
of her stomach wide as Boris's sardonic grin;

suddenly he loathes her; the scene turns grim;
she pleads, begs, kisses his feet, although
she knows they will make love, their limbs a malaise
like tears on a street corner. Despite
all he says, he adores her back, the licentious
way it dips softly and rises like love.

Daniel or Mathieu will find he doesn't love
himself enough to kill himself or face the grim
morning. Someone will have to be deloused.
Boris puts two fingers of water in Pernod although
it makes Ivich wince, and makes Andrée despise
him. The Seine is a crepuscular malaise

at twilight. Through the unending malaise
of Free Will someone will choose to love
the person who at the start they most despised.
A prostitute will have a scar the shape of a grin.
The most idiosyncratic wins, although
he will probably acquire crab lice

in the process. Yet to have crab lice
is a wonderful red badge in the malaise.
Poor Sartre didn't even believe in free will, although
he was admired for trying to love
the great, greasy edges of the Lord's grin.
Many, many will be disillusioned, but despised

is another matter; nobody ever despises
another for more than a candle's second. The lights
blink on and off in their grimaces
and smiles. A hunchback, the Malaysian
drifter who made Marie cry, they love
to show up in the plaza although

they will eventually disappear, lice-ridden and despised.
Although they will represent the lost love,
the solitary grin, the last bolt of light in the malaise.

Dark Matter Theory

They say that only 1% of the galaxy is
made of stars, 5% heavy gases
and planets. Less is garbage dumps
on Rhode Island, gulls crying in compassed

circles, and very little statistically
your stockpile of French-cut
green beans gathering dust as
slowly as the Artic collects snow.

The rest of the *weight of the world*
is unattached subatomic particles, so small they can't
even reflect light. They flow

between us—an ocean
we hardly notice because we are invisible
to most of what is out there. Sometimes a dark matter

particle collides with a visible particle
and the visible particle shakes. Imagine a man losing
his balance and careening

into a small tree. Imagine between each
tree a thousand miles.

In England a team of scientists are
deep in a mine, waiting for one
of these particles to shake an atom of rock.
Standing there, waiting for proof
that we can't even touch

two thirds of the universe;
they're just watching these otherwise useless, nearly
priceless instruments: *O my soul!*

Standard

Like most nights, I was in my favorite bar
sipping a White Russian.
God pulled up a stool and started flirting. I wrote my
       phone number
on a slip of paper and slid it face down across the bar.
       He smiled,
tucked it in his shirt pocket,
then waited three days
before he called, so as not to seem desperate.

Promise My Kidnappers a Seat by My Heart

Before you are born, you are dead.
You are not in Indiana on a Greyhound headed
home for the holidays; you are centerless

as a square without its sides. In desperation,
some passengers drink a bottle of dry
vermouth to keep warm
in this predicament. Others lean

their foreheads against the cold bus window
and forgive themselves, forgive
the bright pinks and greens of their
overdue bills, the Midwest pale

as our organs, each field
of harvested corn, each single-wide
trailer on each hill, the snow
melted above septic tanks.

The bus pulls away, and some
step into the cold in front of the Burlington
Coat Factory and watch people
in the buffet across the street pull

food to their mouths.
The room looks warm as heaven.
Life leaps from dark water.
For others, the used car lots pass, the houses

press together for warmth.
Some passengers are still asleep.
But the unfortunate awake,
privileged enough to think about

the quality and brevity
of life, may find themselves cupping
their hands tightly

as if they were about to carry
a small amount of water across a room.

There's No Common Bond between People

I had the most wonderful night.
A bright-lit café
that bled tables onto the street.
Headlights held long notes, then tailed away.
There was an art fair,
booths come up from the earth
like hell's perfect
elevators. Earlier, my mother
called, said she has two benign tumors
the size of oranges on her ovaries.
I forgot what it was to be *benign*
and stood gripped to my cinderblock wall
and was someone else or possibly
for the first time was me,
huge as that sounds.
Everywhere was music.
A flock of Christians clapping
to a man with an acoustic
guitar and an acoustic soul. Music from
the underage rock club
like the one I used to go to in flannels
and ripped jeans and dumb spectacles
that could only see the present
as an enormous bag
carrying nothing: I can feel
how light my mother will seem
when they take them out.

Untrue Story in a Small Town

In this story I am a high school teacher
in an Indiana town on a river.
I lean on my porch with a sweating
cosmopolitan in a near-dark fiction.
Bats circle an old chimney, and the river, which equals
my real life, threads through the town.
I carry my darkness like a black
doctor's bag, so I am marked as dangerous,
which will intrigue my students, so in the parking lot
one catches my sleeve.
And because in this life my character
is predictable and brave, I put my hand
behind her ear, obscurely, as waking
can be done by dimming the real world. My little house,
shelves, the smell of pine, a girl
who will want to drown what music
has surfaced,
but let me remind you it seems real, brightening
this imaginary autumn on every page;
leaves fall and at one point I
stand in the middle of the football field
at night, so lost and happy in plot,
though it was my intention
to make it rain, I can't pencil in clouds
and bring in life again.

Those Anomalies at a Party When Everyone Suddenly Falls Silent

I love the illustrated medical books
where you can remove the transparencies:
epidermis, muscles, vital organs,
endocrine system, the upside-down
movie screen that hangs on two ropes

in the back of the eye, the skeleton,
until there's just a crude black outline,
empty as a child's résumé. I was pleading
under the eave of the chemistry building,

when someone sapped the lightning
bivouacked in the clouds, burnt
the construction-paper moon, font size
of the rain lessening, until I could barely say,

Please don't leave, don't leave, don't.
Sometimes the silence lasts too long;
something lifts away all the layers until
I'm as empty as that field

by the high school, used for nothing,
but mowed so religiously in the summer.
Then the noise comes back; I watch a plane draw
a chalk line in the sky for God to cross

if he were really here, but the God of jealousy
and wrath must have floated off
in some globular lightning storm to another
universe. In middle school the science

teacher would put up the transparency
of the orbits of the planets,
a big black finger coming in to flip away the earth.

Piranha

I try to tell my students to use images:
                    say, a piranha eating an apple
            or a piranha flying through the air
                                and biting a woman's jugular.

Maybe you could say that when the blood
sprays from the woman's neck it looks like, hmm,
a red Chinese fan.

When I'm asked what a poem should be like,
I simply state the fact that a full-size cow can walk into a river
and a school of piranha can devour it in two minutes.

They work their way into the belly and eat out the soft organs.
Then the skin and head dance on top of the water.

Frank, do all our poems have to be about piranhas?
a student asks—the piranha.
No, no, not if you don't want them to be about piranhas,
I tell her; of course
I really don't see the point
of not writing about piranhas:

that moment when the water starts to break and pop
before the frenzy.

Quitclaim of the Wizard of Oz

Edge of reaped cornfield. Stood there. Dorothy
jump cut–materialized and ran into my arms. "What
happened to the scarecrow?" she asked. "You were
the scarecrow," I replied.
"I knew all along," she said, brushing back her hair.

Dear Anonymous, There are small blue tornadoes
in my eyes when I read your poems about the
outlines of socks on your floor. Your poems entitled
"Depression in a Suitcase."

On 57th Street, Dorothy shook the finches out of her
red scarf. I watched them spiral like a braid of colored
leaves. In the background ran the El. She had a cheese
sandwich. The weather was cold. The edges of her
face looked like a polygraph recording.

Coffee in Greece, heavy grounds at the bottom, the
light from the poem I wrote about watermelons,
the artificial womb of the bathtub, Dorothy's bare
feet out of cuffed jeans; she sat on the edge of the bed,
crossed her legs, and spread out her toes.

Would you trade your lion for courage?

Dear Anonymous, If I were a soldier I'd be a bad
soldier because I wouldn't die for anyone or myself.
May I digress? Black T-Bird blacking out. Yellow
maple tree unzipped. Mattress, independent on
hardwood floor.

What state is shaped like a recovering heart?
What spotlight's directed screaming? What tinge
of happiness as the gale numbs Dorothy's nose in
the Shoe Carnival parking lot?

I put my hands in my hungry pockets. I wink back at the winking moon. Luciferian-covered fingertips lighting the peach hills of Dorothy's eyelids. Rock concert in some apartment clubhouse. Girls Dorothy doesn't know on couches Dorothy doesn't know.

First you'll miss banana shakes in the summertime; then you'll learn we're voices trapped under language. Inside of a cricket is a smaller cricket so it can hear its own intaglio printing, its engraving plates of purple sorrow.

Would you erase the world for a brain?
Would you trade the bashful stars above a field for a heart?

Dorothy has a golden barbecue, and when she grills at night the light waves like the bottom of a swimming pool. The contrast of meat-smells so disturbing. Fire cares little that it's a symbol.

Could you put up with me again, my lazy soldiering, my annoying bullet similes: like the tears of cars, a lost tooth of a metal shark, Death's spit?

Dorothy and I like to be alone in huge spaces, empty big box stores, at the edge of harvested cornfields. I like to feel like the last of my kind.

This is the talking I find significant, talking more like clothing. The broken, frozen reeds of cornstalks, the pale yellow sun struggling to lower its temperature below the silos.

Would you give it all up to go home?

Best Deaths

It is recorded that the happiest
death in history may belong to Chilon
of Sparta, one of the seven sages,
counselor to the king, who enjoyed
walking quietly in the bright sun

of the Peloponnese among the olive
trees. It is possible, even likely, that he stopped
to drag his hand over their leaves.
He was famous for bringing into style the laconic
form of speech, short in utterance

and heavy in meaning, like the very same
trees in fruit. Old and gnarled, it is said
that he actually *died of pride*
in the arms of his son who had just won
an Olympic event. Then he stepped through a door

that got smaller and smaller as he
entered until he was quiet and edgeless
as space. And perhaps he would have kept
the distinction of "best death" except
for Don Doane from Ravenna, Michigan,

who was far from sage, who never predicted
an eclipse that stopped a war, who
was just some guy who bowled
a perfect game for the first time in his life
then promptly died. Don Doane, who

snuffed out his cigarettes on the thin
gold ashtrays, who wasn't the first
to advise "Everything in moderation,"
nor did he visit the oracle at Delphi
and read the words "Know thyself"

and most likely (like you or me) he didn't
know himself very well. At most, maybe,
he wondered in odd moments in the bowling
alley bar when all the pins fell silent
how he even became himself.

The little plastic sword in his
cocktail pierced the heart of the cherry,
and he pulled on his thick gloves
in the silent winter
parking lot to scrape the frost

from his windshield only enough to reach
the light kept on at home. Don Doane,
who knew the universe was a cold place
in which there is little kindness
and fewer gods to bring it,

given only a single mercy—
his friends' images in the buffed floor,
arms raised when the final pins fell.

Train Ride to Yourself in Handcuffs

1.

Nobody will untie you. As the train falls over each
rail and you're jarred to sleep. When you find that
you're the damsel tied to the tracks. As you walk
down the long lines of trees and lampposts

and wake on the same train. Hold on. Stop the poem.

We were both wearing white. The parade went by,
        pinwheels on fire. It was easy
to lean into each other.

The noise from the parade rose forever.

2.

The idea scared the shit out of me. That quite
possibly the world, which I had heretofore
considered only a large and lovely hat,

might be real.

My white sheet looked clear. The Floridians brought
        juice and pills to reduce the fever.
Dreams stood up, lit cigarettes, spoke a word or two
of French and left,
the drapes slowly clucking about the wind.

When I was sleeping the moonless blue

ocean broke off rocks. When I was sleeping
three gold rings were drawn around
the sun at daybreak.

Beads of sweat on my forehead with small anchors in them.

3.

James, me, and the Greek girl with mayonnaised hair. Her
strangely tranquil lapdog. Pay campsites and a fiancé from
India? I couldn't imagine her life.

I nursed my 7:00 a.m. beer and we watched
the ferry dock. And the ocean looked like us all. Free, except
to exist. The ocean looked
like me. The ocean looked like a prison.

4.

Your eyes were blue as a Siberian husky's—*Frank, that is
a Siberian husky.* Oh, but it licked the back of my knee so
gently it could have been a rag of moonlight!

5.

If you're in Toledo clap your hands, in Houston, in San
Diego, and clap your heart at night to stay alive. In history
class so many years ago, at the top of my skull was one
red biplane in an endless loft to my desire.

6.

Half my family is from the South. The only shame
whispered is of Great-Grandfather Trulove, who during the
Depression knelt in a field and took his life with a shotgun.

I hear the echo rolling across the fields and down to the river. A noise, a cloud of blood that must have held itself intact before the wind marched the layers off.

Film Noir

Sunlight broke in the window.
I had the legal right to shoot it and ask questions later.
She stood, hat eclipsing her face. "You've come highly
recommended," she said, more insult than compliment.

This other life is comforting. But in the real world, a more
universal plot brightens. I pull down one shade and focus
on two pans balancing on the cold electric coils of my stove.
I play a few chords on the piano to nobody.

It's only the film that makes the birds black and white,
         abstract, painted in simpler terms.
Able to fly away and flying away.

You see, I'm after what's behind the low-budget scene
where one shadow shoots another, behind what makes
electricity jog around the socket after the power surge.
I dream I have rectangles of skin stapled over my skin.

As if I'm trapped under some artifice and can't surface.
I confirmed my suspicions: One day I found the rain was
just someone spraying a hose against the window, the
thunder just a big sheet of metal.

I'll be driving down 37 in Indiana and exit on 154th Street
in the Bronx, fifty years ago, holding up a picture at a gas
station: "Have you seen this lady, a black Oldsmobile?"
I polish my telephoto lens with a handkerchief as the
cheating husband leans in the door of the hotel for a last
kiss. I don't care if she looks as fresh as a cherry pie cooling
on the windowsill for a starving god of cliché; she fits well
on a negative that will develop into a positive on adultery.

Heaven's a difficult place to get into, but it's an open-book
test. You can bring one note card written on front and back.

God is kind. Explain the missile, heatstroke, Greek
food. But walking from the car to the Kmart, I feel as
if I'm in some lower house of heaven, as if a hand
might pull out the keystone and everything, and the
everything behind everything will blink into rain.

Most of the work isn't exciting. My date tonight is
the bottom forth of a fifth of rye whiskey. In the
film, a woman in a long coat runs down to the bay,
says, "The sky is an old book of names," seemingly
to no one.

In the Blue Garter, the jewel-eyed singer visits each
mobster's table, picks up their chins with her gloved
hand but secretly glances at me, who knows form
and fulfillment. Say it starts to rain. A silhouette
darkens the soaped glass of my office and my
cigarette brightens my face.

"It was raining. I had to come in," she says.
And from that moment I know she's behind the
brightness, so I unfold the light in the room and
unfold my legs off the table, and lean forward into
the unfolded light, and we unfold a few words,
and she unfolds her hands.

You see, light goes out and out until my heart is lit
up like a truck stop, until I feel like a detective who
has forgotten why he was jaded, who has only the
wardrobe to inform him that trust was never part
of the job.

The films are beautiful. But some mornings, in the
real world, I'm afraid something was set in motion
by these people a long time ago. I can see by the
way they hold hands out at the harbor. There is

something unsettling about the door left open, a brief shot
of a match floating in a cup of coffee,

the boat lights tacked to the sea at night with butterfly pins.

One Last Waltz on an Ave Maria

If there was music in your life, on that beach, if the
wind worked the sand into loops before it pulled out
the first stitch into the dark. We ran cords and portable
heaters from the house to warm our legs. There's a
picture I remember somewhere east, a hook of trees
around a pond.

When I came home I expected to see snow, for things
to be covered, for my age, the passing of years to be
glorified by a gifted underneath that when the thaw
comes would shine again. The dilapidated garage,
the alley baked in snow.

Baby trains cry in the distance.

Goldenrod bent to forward slashes. Sparrows thrown
        like handfuls of mud from one power line to
        the next.
What little I had.
Each gravel driveway frozen in its flow to the street.

Been praying over a jar of Miracle Whip?

I'll give you another option in a black cloak with a
sickle, with a penchant for chess, who fogs under cars,
whose shoulders are road snow: Someone is painting
you in his memory with no objective craft at all.

The plane high above, its cold comet's tail. It could
be the first plane. Leaves blown into large curled
hands. Imagine a movie from the seventies, the
saturated color; the men wear corduroy and beards,
are athletic in a lanky way, fall in love with girls who
wear no bras, whose nipples point through white
blouses and whose hair falls straight. Faces mangled
and attractive.

There are so many things I remember about this life. A
ceiling of winter clouds above the outdoor theater. A case
of bottled beer between us. Poorly tended fire. Draw an
outline around your reflection in the mirror so someone
knows you died there.

In your oven is a smaller, warmer eternity. God in his pillar.
The ubiquitous woman on a lawn chair. History lesson
number one: Each daybreak comes.

You'll have children, and they'll seem too heavy even at
birth to carry the weight of birth. You'll fill the bath on a
cold night and sweat, sad to know there was a time in your
life when something was decided.

Leaning closer and closer.

As if you were moving into the past, leaves unpile across
the yard, backflip through the air, lucky and mad and hook
their leeches' mouths on the trees, grow smaller. What
appears to move backward is your failure to feel your life
grow solid, your inability to simply reel.

Frost weighing down the blades of grass. A giant American
            flag over an outlet mall.

Reflected on my glasses, images of things starving and cold,
high-tension wires hiss and divide the chalk-blue winter sky
into highways. The little dog looks out at the wires,
trying to pinpoint the sound. I should have pitied him,
but only something more refined remembers.

We stood in the center of my room; each light from the
            small mirror ball was a ring of desire's despotism.
The room is spinning again.

Beware the dubious patriotism of the baseball bat
and the Devil and the rhubarb pie.

The way months halo around a baby's brain and
darken the edges until twenty years later she can
watch a crow glide by the fifth-story window and
almost come to grips with the legend of the failure
of the great light-producing machine.

A few old trailers sunk into the sides of hills.

It's not easy to believe the world is real. A significant
relationship problem: can't commit metaphysically.
Not afraid to cry; maybe cries too much. Preheated
to 98.7 degrees. Can see the solution to a maze in a dog.

Strange the silence without the roar of cars and
trains and planes, mating and fighting cats,
corrugated roofs, midpoints of tumbleweeds, steam
from sewer grates, steel that smiles, sun through the
windows in the state courthouse rotunda.
Eventually I'll strip down to my bones.

Won't I look funny then? Won't I be difficult to rob,
to stab? Sometimes when I'm sleeping I start falling
through the bed through the night, my clothes
outstretched like flags, hair raised from static.

Imagine a beach, someplace in your memory hazy
enough for meaning, blurred enough to be emotion
itself stretching into the curve of the horizon, all that
dark inside lifted somehow into the laugh lines of
waves, the one or two logs bloating at the high-tide
mark, the sheen of the new night sky, that when you
look back at your life, it will seem almost as if
nothing was there.

Leaning closer and closer.

We were sixteen and pulled off on Southport Road because our song came on. It comes on and on again, the memory loss, the days grayed and lost, the pit of tar in a glance, the careful art of revolution in a smile, one second that murders the one before with a candlestick in a room that's off the board.

Every time I think of that scene more appears, one more shadow of a raindrop on the dash, a heaviness in the air, a square of skin on my arm at cold attention, deep as a mistake. Did I love you when I knew we would become other people? Noise shot through the hands of maple leaves. Over the dead cornfields.

One day, and this hurts to talk about, while walking through the long practice field to high school I looked up at the gray winter Indiana sky

and I opened. And for the first time I knew I'd never be
        myself again.
The something now a *someone in me*.

We pulled off the road to kiss when our song came on. The sun pulled under the cornfield, and the night and rain came down thick. A helix of noise swung around the TV tower. I almost stopped! I could see noise! Noise powered from the stereo clock's blue bones. Hurtling my silver fillings, light from the utility trail, lives in the shadows on the dash.

The windshield began to fog. I put my mouth to yours to move it into the shape of what I needed to say: There would be no end to our losing, our falling, to the beach, to the gulls in the darkening sky, to waking every morning into the same suit of skin.

That night in the car I lost the world.

****

Many years have passed since that night. And I've
learned a rhythm to my days. That waking up in-
volves flipping the numerator over the denominator.
That if I catch the sun at the right angle it looks as if
I've been painted by an artist who can't sleep because
the sound of pipes at night makes him feel as if he's
in the belly of a half-imagined animal. And he is.

God help me and forgive me. I was there and I wasn't
there. Forgive me; I was there and I wasn't wholly
there. Forgive me for being there. Lights of planes
move across the sky, each somnolent light drug-slow.

Forgive the movement and the copilot and the flying.
Forgive who turned up the volume of the snow.
Forgive the soldiers, who were told to fire when they
saw the whites of eyes because there was still some
idea of heaven in war, of salvation. A storm

of white seeds came down over the polished hoods
of new Mercedes. I remember a rock club with a big
metal dragon that shot fire over the heads of the
crowd, lighting their faces in an underworldly gold,
row upon row, beautiful and frightened, each lit
from within by their own separate purgatories, their
separation and the closure of themselves—save me
also,

that when I pray, I whisper, so no one but you can
hear me, for at times when I lace my hands together
to open the line it seems the biggest betrayal to ask

for another world,

another life.

When You Left I Started a Garden

After I drank so much my name was lifted
from my body on a white string

and my lungs were black as soil,
I started growing

tomatoes in the kitchen, beans
lining the rails,

a lime tree in a huge ceramic pot
the weight and texture of an old stone anger,

and a pomegranate tree to remind me
not to look back.

I tore up half the yard
to plant radishes, cauliflower, cucumbers,

kale; some of the seeds
are so small they look like dust (thyme,
rosemary), empty

soup cans overflowing with parsley.

And when I found an old statue of *The Birth
of Venus* standing alone

in an alley by someone's trash, I picked
her up and carried her

four blocks, stood her by the wall
and draped tomato vines over her arms.

I can see her from my window at night

always emerging from
the delinquent froth of empty air,
riding a shell.

Faking It

My girlfriend has multiple orgasms.
I'm not sure who is giving
her these orgasms, but she'll come home with
a grocery sack and drop them on the table—

they look like tiny doorknobs made of bronze.
Neither of us is sure how they move:
They start floating in random directions
through the air, the ceiling, clouds.

Stepping out of the shower,
she's beautiful. Though
if she weren't an art
so much my creation, I don't think
I'd love her at all.

At the industrial coffee shop,
three packets of sugar: One leans against
a white mug, another the silver napkin
dispenser, and one faints

on the table
like a simplistic murder scene.

My mind goes places not quite thought
on cool spring mornings
when all my little infidelities
float off above the trees.

Quick Study in Unhappiness

There's a light
directly above my head
in this café, as if I have an idea.
I have no idea.
In thirty years, I have
barely managed to watch the snow
collect on the uncollected
phone books on my porch.
Once, I suspected it all
may have to stop, the people,
trains crossing the country,
and I wouldn't have to feel anymore.
Every month the wind
sweeps through my paycheck.
I have a cat left over
from a previous girlfriend. It's
like a little memory
that naps three quarters
of its life. It stretches
out on the carpet which still
holds the blood and ash
of the last tenants. It would sleep
on my coffin if the sun
were on it. Once I had
the idea that I might
be unhappy. Soon unhappiness
draped over the trees
like mosquito netting. I could
hum it in the shower.
Snow all week, says the weather
man. The blue tint freezing
him in the television.

Vegas Lights, Hedge Funds, Monetary Policy and Beauty

In the hotel room, dust, ground
from the edges of the long run,
blew under the door. Swimming

pool flush as we slipped in.
Heat detectors swung
overhead without a sound.

I wished then I could turn to your body
and the odds
would come off with your clothes.

There used to be an old kind of sadness
a mom-and-pop sadness,
a sadness you could hold in your

hands as you buckled over
on the curb and took off your hat, warm,

heavy as a wadded nocturne,
that slowed the passing memories
just enough to feel as if you

could go back if the wind were slight
and westerly. But the new sadness
is monetized.
It knows what we can afford.

I'm for hedging
my bets. Look at me, downright distrustful
of beauty, how it locks the risk from the dice—

what should be among us, condensed
in even features—ten thousand
ships etc., a sea etc.,

I haven't been the first to question

why we are so wild for something easy
as the clean architecture of a face.

Yet when you slipped into the pool
something clean and brutal
possessed me: I was embarrassed
at being like everyone else.
For you see, I have this secret dream,

almost the opposite song of the soul,
I feel blow through me,
a bright string, where the one

who makes the beauty, the
queen behind
the universe shivers,
                    and for a moment drops her spade.

Salutatorian's Speech

My grandfather was a fire-
fighter. He died and they kept
delivering the paper

in its orange jacket
to his doorstep like a tiny
afterlife. He told me a story:

He pulled on a woman's
arm and it came off. The theme
of this speech is loss. Theme

is what you carry
away while the body turns
to ash. The little iron shovel

by the fireplace, the black
construction paper, the stars
on strings of a grade school

play, the rumormonger
bumblebees floating
like fat starships over

the peonies. Theme orders it all,
sets your calculator
on quotient for lust, smell

of jasmine, taste of a quince,
makes the I-beams act
self-important. And then

in the June-heavy rain you fall
in love with the witchcraft
that knits brake lights together.

Theme selects the varsity
moments in our lives when something
happens quick and distinct
as the sound of a ring box

closing. The sun rises, the moon,
some other celestial crap. But, no, my
speech tonight is about

my neighbor, a grown man sobbing
in the courtyard under the palm tree.
A diabetic and an alcoholic,

he will be dead in a few weeks.
Like a plane, he has a black box
in his head that he can't break

to obscure the tapes. I'll watch them
carry him out on a stretcher
as if being displayed one

last time to the world.
Brave means dealing
with pain; thin means carrying little

with you. The mouse
has it right: It is the single gray bag
it carries. Who am I kidding;

this speech is about how
it crosses my mind in the odd
moment, say, watching

the little flakes
of tinfoil in the surf, how I want to skin
the night to see its system

of propulsion, how the trick may be
to paint over in huge black
strokes, infinite pieces of competent

artistry to get at a single
important pain. Franklin Central
High School Class of 1997! Future

bullies, barmaids, doctors,
inmates, interns, oh, you want to be alive.
Be careful of your success.

Concerto Pour la Main Gauche

I'm listening to the *Concerto*
for the Left Hand that Ravel
wrote for Wittgenstein, not Ludwig,
but his brother, the concert

pianist, who lost his right arm
in the First World War. The song
is bold and fast, showing strength
of the remaining function,

no doubt a demonstration of national
Austrian pride, but no matter
how skilled, it is hard to cloak the fact
that the song was built around absence.

My stepfather has this nightmare
about a pair of polished black shoes,
alone in a whitish, ethereal plane.
It's not that the shoes are

conspicuously empty that wakes
him—it is that in an uncanny
moment they begin walking.
Sometimes I hear the right hand

playing beyond authorship, and it
keeps me awake at night.
I live by the beach, and the waves,
almost like concurrent knives,

strike the dark. And I think of
the summer I broke down, convinced
the world might be a spoon in
a Rube Goldberg machine,

walking the scrub brush beyond
the stables, feeling something too
verdant, too overgrown in
the landscape, how the grass-

hoppers were large and brown
and looked like keys.

Inventors of Sadness Learn to Use What They Have the Wrong Ways

Bereft of injury, bad parenting, civil war,
death in the family, extreme phobias,
psychological trauma,
not convinced I was abducted in some field
in Iowa and told the golden truth of the world.

Having sidestepped the factories of brutal
poverty, the Midwest, not attaching
the same part to the same part.

Tomorrow, bicycles maybe by the Spree!
Having partaken of petting
the fat underbelly of a puppy,
living in a democracy of sorts.

Living in an apartment where the cherry trees
in Mauer Park blow their
leaves up pale and pink past

my window like eraser dust—
everything reduced
to brightness, nights blooming quietly,
Yvonne twisting in the sheets,
the moon safely nailed to sky.

And the man across the courtyard
plays the piano, slow, Chopin's
Nocturne in C Minor I think,

and the wind touches the leaves
of the trees so softly
I barely hear them shake. Yes, no one knows
I am the Edison of my day,

dumpy in my chair by the window,
that with only a few regrets, a lost love
or two for gears, that tonight

I have done it!
From almost nothing at all:

I have found a way to be unhappy.

I Want to Steal Your Girlfriend, Michael Grady

I'm watching her hand already,
slender but muscled by the bar light,
and I feel all the clichés about love
rubbing their hands around a barrel fire

eager to trek out one more time
into that cold night. And there you are,
Mike Grady, looking into your bourbon
as if you lost something

in its fog. Outside, she trudges through
the snow, mittens clipped to her coat.
Streetlight and moonlight,
a lacquer that quiets the town.

The courthouse wrapped in dead
Christmas lights. The shops exhausted
after being warmed all day
like little ovens. No sounds of cars, just light

settling to gold dust in the snow. And,
how expert we have become
at standing forever
back from the things we want!

These are the thoughts that get me slapped.

But *divinity of Hell!* All is fair
in love and war they say because under
our hearts are rooms of pure brutality
so bright and industrious, so much

the substance of steel, when the metal works
open in the brightness and flush
forgive us, but it's hard to pin
down exactly what our loyalties are *for*.

Regret Bishop

I'm afraid this line has been played.
There are certain recognizable openings,
defenses:

the sepia photograph of you
standing by the fence in the western
dust, gutted under the musk

of saguaro flowers. This is the story

of a strategy, our sort-of successful life,
the flowering newsprint
across the kitchen table, the "newsy"
flowers, the bats above the parking lot lights
signing off on the night.

When I lived in sad Indianapolis,
I loved to walk across the high school
football field on October mornings
after the first warm snow

to feel held for a moment in the brig
of brightness, among the traitors,
the optics shattered in heaven—

everything new! I didn't know sacrifice,
how it dwindles to kings
and an empty board and most days
you feel only like a rhetorical

someplace. But oh, my ode to Basho
and the cold comb under his heel; I wasn't
expecting it, a peaceful morning:
the coffee cup warm between my hands

against the snow-thick sky. This cup
was once yours, ours, from what
bevel, what blindspot, what immaculate

almost religious gambit did you
sweep in to take me?

Introduction to Archery

At the end of *The Odyssey*
only Odysseus has the strength
to string his bow and fire
an arrow through the handles of twelve

axes. And in the end he kills all
the suitors. The poor suitors
who would have certainly said,
"Sorry, man. You understand," and slapped

Odysseus on his shoulder
while gathering up their bows
if Odysseus had just walked
in the fucking front door. Instead, they crowd

Penelope like a Renaissance
painting where everyone is frozen
in a massive thrust, clambering
over one another in military charges

or to touch the body of Christ.
This was humanity then, polyphonic.
They understood a certain
amount of collateral

damage; there was no god
from the machine, as when Athena
simply erases the anger from the minds
of the townspeople, easily as

wiping down a chalkboard, so they
abandon retaliation against Odysseus
for hacking the young men of Ithaca
to bits for petty slights. I'm getting

nervous, my peach, that something
in the core of desire is rotten,
the seed itself. *There there*, you say,

and place an apple from the fridge
against my head to cool me down.

Last Poem in a Book

What the lord giveth the lord
taketh away: He's a real
ass that way—always acting
like your mother, calling you
from the living with that voice
used when you forgot your chores,
or sticking you in a cloud
for no reason, no good reason!
No blackberries or black
licorice, no more moments
on a cliff side. I like
the Ptolemaic view of
the heavens with Earth
as the center of corruption
refined through every sphere,
until on the final track—
the purest music, like
the ambient sound on
the last inch of a record.
I'd rather clap along
with that tune than think of
space; I know I sound high
when I say we're all small,
but cut me some slack, it's hard
to laugh off after a while.
But I've been
trying. I've been trying
when I go to the beach
at night and hear it knock
on the land, to get comfortable
with leaving this world, this
ocean, these trees, the long
wheat grass, having hardly
touched a thing.

Demolition

I feel good today, as if I'm stealing God's cable.
Everything is full of color, firmly etched.
Every sparrow feels thoroughly "watched,"
judgmental but a little lazy,

not kicking stones or whistling,
content to walk through the world
unseen. Last night I had a dream
that I could see close up
and far away, but the middle ranges

were a blur. Being outer-sighted,
it was hard to see the drama, the stage,
while the rafters and my hands
were so clear. I reacted clumsily.

The audience laughed, embarrassed;
I was angry. A jealous god
would punish their children
and their children's children for old sins, throw
out bitter storms, shake

the earth like a petulant child because
his fingers are too fat for the delicate
surgery of revenge, the little cutting
words we say to each other with such

an art they remove an exact
building in the city of the heart. God
doesn't make buildings come down
in exact controlled plumes

of dust, leaving the surrounding
buildings untouched; those flowers,
those are ours.

Blackout Chef

I had a friend whose father,
every night after coming home
from looking for work,
would sit down at the kitchen
table and with medical accuracy

pour six shots of vodka
into six glasses and drink them
one per minute. Then he
would stand, open a bottle of wine

and start cooking in his little
basement apartment,
which he rented after the divorce,
until his memory lifted away.

Starved of himself,
he grew so hungry
he would prepare elaborate
meals: New York strip steaks

a perfect medium,
roasted lamb with rosemary
and mint, tomato
and cilantro gazpacho.

He must have staggered through
the bright aisles of the grocery
rooting around the crisper
for kale while Sheryl Crow

played overhead, or slurred to
the manager about the lack
of fresh tarragon. In his bright warm
kitchen with the snow piled

above the basement windows
in the winter months when the sun
would set at five p.m., he pulled his face
from the steam of the pots,

wrinkled in an expression
of joy in preparing things
that made sense, but the next morning,
he would wake to find it all there

untouched, gleaming on plates,
his night work, having appeared seemingly
from nowhere—from someone

who had the things he lacked in life:
taste, inspiration,
the power
to wake up the next morning,

someone else.

Object Permanence and the U.S. Postal Service

I like hotel beds with the sheets
tucked tight, so it feels as if I'm falling
asleep in a huge white envelope.

Most days I'm sorry
that I'm sent away.

I admire the half-erased
equations still visible

on the chalkboards on campus,
and it feels as if I'm standing
two feet under my life.

When I was twenty-two, I thought
there was no math

behind the universe.
I would watch a red-winged blackbird
on a fence post

until my eyes watered up.
My sadness felt like a lodger
entering a Norwegian cabin
unlacing his boots

and sitting quietly by a fire.
I tried to keep it inside,

these *undeliverables*, but at parties
the chaos under it
all became too muscular to ignore,
and one night I began yelling, "There's nothing

below us, nothing!" and my
friends dragged me out
under the rented night.

In my upstairs room, shaking,
my heart sounded like the applause
when a group of birds
flies away. Maybe carrier

pigeons or doves
from a top hat, or from the palms
of an unwitting assistant.

But I don't trust magicians.
I get nervous when things just appear

behind capes. When I was a baby,
my mother's face would appear

from behind her hands.

Your mother is here; your mother is gone.
Your mother is here; your mother is gone.

Viticulture

I am drinking a fifty-five-dollar bottle of wine by myself.
It's delicious

being by myself.

It was a very good year

for the wine.
I can taste it, the fullness and sun
from another season.

The timing of the harvest,
nothing left

past due, not too sweet
or tannic,
taken the very moment it was perfect

and crushed. I'm old enough
to appreciate

there may never be another
cruelty so sweet—

snow almost warm now
in my memory,
the first heartbreak

grown more full each year.

Death of the Stranger

On the cruise ship to St. Croix your eyeliner

looked like the silhouette of a woman

draped over a small hill. I smiled, and in my

left eye a candle flame flickered. It didn't

take long to kill the stranger, to procure

a yard of deck rope and strangle him

by the grumpy engine under the big rivets.

We dumped him, and his black heft slapped the sea.

Somehow we'd never get caught; somehow

the stranger was a stranger to everyone.

On deck, you wore that lovely fire-printed,

backless dress and I my fine purple scarf—it was done.

I held my martini glass high so

the moon floated on top as we toasted.

They Did It to Us and We Loved Them for Doing It So Hard

Degenerate to the end we felt at home,
almost conservative, begging
as they pulled handfuls of
string from our stomachs.

Defrauder we screamed to egg them on.
Each cold-hearted breach, frost, ice,
itchy stitches, everything but order—
common to connect with the oppressor.

They dissolved us from August
nights, thin, easy. Due to the
concomitant divorce we were scared, but
we kept swimming. I hate

that I have to die. Can't be a vein
in a dimmer flower. The thumbscrew,
smiles, the sex, bodies washed,
unwashed, how subtly the bandage
becomes centerless. We love

how they look down like scholars
at the flaw in us. Butcher. The tent
thrown up so quick, tax,
temperature in summer. We knew it
was stuck on good, and we begged them
to pull it off slow.

Like autumn *heals* the trees.
They hit us on the nose, "the prominent
part of the human face." They listened
to nothing and limited everything.
Gladiatorial light wept at their feet.

We cheered it on, threw our betting
slips down in a pink rain; they
made a lobby in our bodies, a hotel in our lives.
We endorsed each encroachment

as the imp. They struck thousands
off the ledger at birth. Almost
no accounting. And what spousal feelings we had

listening to the thrum at the tops of trees,
chorus above cruelty, momentarily,
but came back to the job, the self,
the pinpoint.

They beat us the way rain beats a roof,
and we asked for it again and again.

A Time to Sing of Airports

Before I taxi and lift away—
I'd like to touch you, drag a ring finger
up your forearm, kiss the back of your ear.
We enter moonlight like a loose door—

I mean, tonight I saw a piece of old flat gum
dark gray on the sidewalk—
a terribly insignificant moment—

my whole life. The moon so bright, clear,
and just in that point of the desert sky
it could have been the sequestered heart
of an invisible giant. Before I carry

farther to that place, I'd like to touch you,
drag my tongue up the washboard
on the roof of your mouth. I comfort
myself on the plane by finding

the meanest-looking old man and thinking,
If God takes me, he takes him too. And those
people don't die in plane wrecks;
they just evaporate from hospital beds,

the IV still swaying. There's a time to sing
about umbrellas, and a time to scream
in the rain and pound on the diner window
and beg someone to hear you.

Midflight I worry
that if I imagined something never thought of,
say, a tiny Arabian horse in a light bulb,
that I'd accidentally trigger some ancient hex

that would shut off all machinery, plane engines,
a divine punishment for originality, a
humbling force. But the plane goes on with or
without my imagination, and the tear

slides down the nectarine, and I look at
the rooftops and know it's not
about rooftops or empty theater seats
or wearing the same pair of jeans so long
they can walk into a bar themselves

and start a fight. The *No Smoking* icon dings.
Here is the lighted tennis court, here
the mouse in its panicked constitution,
here, my own blessed socks passed out on the floor,

drunk with smell. Know, before I leave
I'd like to touch you, because miles below us
they're turning off the lights in the city
and it has been so long
since you've been touched.

Gratuitous Voice-Over at the End of a Film, Reflecting on the Tribulations of the Plot and Coming Finally to an Epiphany

Then I realized, rowing across the lake,
that even if Mother never leaves the sanitarium
and they build another aviary and free the bullfinches
like drops of yellow paint into the sky,
the sun survives; and if Steven gets another postcard
from some port from a sailor who might be
his father, and if Jessica decides to forgive me for my
            comment
in the lighthouse as our silhouettes were broadcast
like two conjoined giants on the midnight-purple sea,
and if we recover the petrified cat
from the soup and ash of the house;
if all this were to happen,
rowing across this lake with the trees in their
last struggle of color as the cold opens a hole in the sky
and the water hardens to glass—
I thought about Charles at the Café de Flore
smoking Gauloises and watching the ankles of girls
young as blue flowers; the world never runs out,
though we choose someone to love above the rest
and get down to defining or dying—
Claire and the shining
woman alighting from the jewelry store,
winter rain cutting through tree branches,
all this inevitable turning in my life,
a tornado kicking out shreds of barn,
or an icebreaker ship rolling like an oily bell.
It's as if there's a camera that pans out farther
and farther until you question what holds it.
Then I realized, rowing across the lake,
that there's so little to keep me from sinking,
just this small craft,
suspended above the consuming water.

Acknowledgments

Several of these poems appeared in the chapbook *A Civic Pageant*, published by Black Lawrence Press, which won the 2007 Black River Chapbook Contest.

Vertebrae: "Introduction to Archery"

Sixth Finch: "Salutatorian's Speech" and "Standard"

La Fovea: "*Concerto Pour la Main Gauche*" and "Last Poem in a Book"

Crescent City Review: "I Want to Steal Your Girlfriend, Michael Grady" and "Demolition"

Tin House: "Quick Study in Happiness"

Black Warrior Review: "Every 1930s French Novel"

Spork: "Heaven's Undershirt," "Train Ride to Yourself in Handcuffs," "One Last Waltz on an Ave Maria," "Inventors of Sadness Learn to Use What They Have the Wrong Ways," and "Blackout Chef"

Poet Lore: "Quitclaim of the Wizard of Oz"

Nimrod: "Piranha"

Cream City Review: "Gratuitous Voice-Over at the End of a Film Reflecting on the Tribulations of the Plot and Coming Finally to an Epiphany"

Green Mountain Review: "The Incalculably Long Geometry of Sobriety"

Harness: "Untrue Story in a Small Town"

Alaska Quarterly Review: "Redundancy of Light" and "Dark Matter Theory"

Barrow Street: "Faking It"

42Opus: "A Flock of Iagos Waiting in the Wings"

DIAGRAM: "Those Anomalies at Parties When Everyone Falls Silent"

Poems and Plays: "Film Noir"

Lit: "There's No Common Bond between People"

Slipstream: "A Time to Sing of Airports"

Cavalier: "Vegas Lights," "Hedge Funds," Monetary Policy," and "Beauty"

Thanks to the many people who helped me through versions of this book, in particular, Joshua Marie Wilkinson, Sommer Browning, James Meetze, Tony Mancus, Hannah Hass, Sophie Sills, Ben Garceau, Matthew Sadler, Michael Rerick, Melissa Koosmann and the rest of the Arizona crew. Thanks to my teachers, Abner Bartequez and Brian Teare, for their early encouragement. Special thanks to the late Jon Anderson. Time and support for writing this collection was given by the Jay Tanner McClurg Summer Fellowship, and the Tim and Ken Writer's Retreat. And, of course, thanks to my friends and family.

Frank Montesonti is the author of the chapbook *A Civic Pageant* (Black Lawrence Press, 2009). He has been published in literary journals such as *Tin House*, *Black Warrior Review*, *AQR*, *Poet Lore*, and *Poems and Plays*, among many others. *Blight, Blight, Blight, Ray of Hope* is his first full-length collection. His second collection, *Hope Tree*, is forthcoming from Black Lawrence Press in 2014. He has an MFA from the University of Arizona and teaches poetry at National University. A longtime resident of Indiana, he now lives in Los Angeles, California.

Barrow Street Poetry

Blight, Blight, Blight, Ray of Hope
Frank Montesonti (2012)

Self-evident
Scott Hightower (2012)

Emblem
Richard Hoffman (2011)

Mechanical Fireflies
Doug Ramspeck (2011)

Warranty in Zulu
Matthew Gavin Frank (2010)

Heterotopia
Lesley Wheeler (2010)

This Noisy Egg
Nicole Walker (2010)

Black Leapt In
Chris Forhan (2009)

Boy with Flowers
Ely Shipley (2008)

Gold Star Road
Richard Hoffman (2007)

Hidden Sequel
Stan Sanvel Rubin (2006)

Annus Mirabilis
Sally Ball (2005)

A Hat on the Bed
Christine Scanlon (2004)

Hiatus
Evelyn Reilly (2004)

3.14159+
Lois Hirshkowitz (2004)

Selah
Joshua Corey (2003)